The Dollar's Decline: How the Shift in Oil Payments Impacts the U.S. Economy

Copyright Page

TITLE: The Dollar's Decline: How the Shift in Oil Payments Impacts the U.S. Economy

1ST Edition

Copyright @ 2023

Roberto M. Rodriguez. All rights reserved.

ISBN: 9798223902485

Table of Contents

The Dollar's Decline: How the Shift in Oil Payments Impacts the U.S. Economy

By Roberto Miguel Rodriguez

Description of the Book

The book, "The Dollar's Decline: How the Shift in Oil Payments Impacts the U.S. Economy," aims to address economists and politicians. The book explores the potential consequences and implications of the world's oil no longer being paid with U.S. dollars but with other currencies.

The book includes the following subtopics:

1. What Happens to the U.S. Economy when the World's Oil is No Longer Paid with U.S. Dollars But With Other Currencies?

- Understanding the current system of oil payments and its reliance on the U.S. dollar.

- Analyzing the potential impact on the U.S. economy when oil payments shift to other currencies.

- Exploring the challenges and opportunities that arise from this shift.

2. Impact on the U.S. Dollar Value: Analyzing the Effect of Shifting Oil Payments on the Value of the U.S. Dollar and Its Position as a Global Reserve Currency.

- Examining the historical relationship between oil payments and the value of the U.S. dollar.

- Assessing the potential consequences of a decline in the U.S. dollar's status as the dominant currency for oil payments.

- Analyzing the implications for the U.S. economy and global financial markets.

3. Geopolitical Implications: Examining the Potential Consequences on U.S. Foreign Relations and Global Power Dynamics When Oil is No Longer Paid in U.S. Dollars.

- Assessing the potential impact on U.S. foreign policy and global alliances.

- Examining the geopolitical implications of a shift in oil payments away from the U.S. dollar.

- Analyzing the potential consequences for U.S. influence and global power dynamics.

4. Energy Independence and Alternative Fuels: Exploring How the Shift Away from Oil Payments in U.S. Dollars Could Incentivize the U.S. to Develop Alternative Energy Sources and Reduce Dependence on Oil.

- Assessing the potential for increased investment in alternative energy sources.

- Analyzing the implications for U.S. energy independence and national security.

- Exploring the economic opportunities and challenges associated with transitioning to alternative fuels.

5. Trade Balance and Current Account Deficit: Investigating the Impact on the U.S. Trade Balance and Current Account Deficit When Oil Payments are No Longer Denominated in U.S. Dollars.

- Analyzing the potential effects on U.S. trade flows and balance of payments.

- Assessing the consequences for the U.S. current account deficit.

- Exploring strategies to mitigate any negative impact on the U.S. economy.

6. Inflation and Consumer Prices: Analyzing the Potential Effects on Inflation and Consumer Prices in the U.S. as a Result of Changing Oil Payment Currencies.

- Assessing the relationship between oil prices, inflation, and consumer prices.

- Analyzing the potential impact on inflation and consumer purchasing power.

- Exploring potential policy responses to mitigate any adverse effects.

7. Stock Market and Investment Implications: Examining the Potential Consequences on U.S. Stock Markets and Investment Flows When the World's Oil is No Longer Paid in U.S. Dollars.

- Assessing the potential impact on U.S. stock markets and investment flows.

- Analyzing the implications for domestic and international investors.

- Exploring strategies to maintain market stability and attract investment.

8. Federal Reserve and Monetary Policy: Analyzing the Role of the Federal Reserve in Managing the U.S. Economy During the Transition to Alternative Oil Payment Currencies.

- Examining the challenges faced by the Federal Reserve in managing monetary policy during the transition.

- Assessing the potential impact on interest rates, money supply, and exchange rates.

- Exploring potential policy responses to ensure economic stability during the transition.

9. Energy Sector Restructuring: Exploring the Potential Changes in the U.S. Energy Sector and Investment Patterns Resulting from Shifting Oil Payment Currencies.

- Examining the implications for the U.S. energy sector and related industries.

- Assessing the potential for investment reallocation and restructuring.

- Exploring the opportunities for job creation and economic growth in alternative energy sectors.

10. Economic Sanctions and Global Influence: Examining How the Use of Alternative Oil Payment Currencies Could Impact the Effectiveness of U.S. Economic Sanctions and Its Global Influence.

- Analyzing the potential consequences for U.S. sanctions and their efficacy.

- Assessing the impact on U.S. global influence and diplomatic relations.

- Exploring potential strategies to maintain influence and address geopolitical challenges.

11. Currency Wars and Financial Instability: Investigating the Potential Risks and Challenges Posed by a Shift Away from the U.S. Dollar as the Dominant Currency for Oil Payments, Including Currency Wars and Financial Instability.

- Assessing the risks associated with currency wars and financial instability.

- Analyzing the potential consequences for global financial markets and stability.

- Exploring policy responses to mitigate risks and promote stable international monetary system.

Chapter 1: Introduction

Background and significance of the topic

In recent years, there has been growing speculation and concern about the potential shift away from the U.S. dollar as the dominant currency for oil payments. This shift, if it were to occur, would have significant implications for the U.S. economy, global power dynamics, and the world financial system. As economists and politicians, it is crucial to understand and analyze the potential consequences and opportunities that arise from this shift.

One of the key areas to explore is the impact on the U.S. dollar value. Analyzing the effect of shifting oil payments on the value of the U.S. dollar and its position as a global reserve currency is essential. A decline in the demand for dollars could lead to a depreciation of the currency, affecting trade balances and creating challenges for the Federal Reserve in managing monetary policy.

The geopolitical implications of this shift cannot be ignored. Examining the potential consequences on U.S. foreign relations and global power dynamics when oil is no longer paid in U.S. dollars is crucial. This change could potentially weaken the influence of the United States and reshape the global economic and political landscape.

Furthermore, the shift away from oil payments in U.S. dollars could incentivize the U.S. to develop alternative energy sources and reduce dependence on oil. Exploring how this shift could impact energy independence and alternative fuels is necessary to understand the potential opportunities and challenges for the U.S. energy sector.

The impact on the U.S. trade balance and current account deficit is another important area to investigate. When oil payments are no longer denominated in U.S. dollars, there could be significant changes in trade patterns and imbalances, which would have implications for the overall health of the U.S. economy.

Additionally, it is crucial to analyze the potential effects on inflation and consumer prices in the U.S. as a result of changing oil payment currencies. Changes in oil payment currencies could have indirect effects on consumer prices and inflation, which would impact the purchasing power of individuals and the overall stability of the economy.

Examining the potential consequences on U.S. stock markets and investment flows when the world's oil is no longer paid in U.S. dollars is also essential. This shift could lead to significant changes in investment patterns and investor sentiment, impacting the overall performance of the U.S. stock market.

Finally, understanding the role of the Federal Reserve in managing the U.S. economy during the transition to alternative oil payment currencies is crucial. Analyzing the potential challenges and opportunities for the Federal Reserve and its monetary policy is necessary to ensure a smooth transition and manage any potential risks.

Overall, the shift away from the U.S. dollar as the dominant currency for oil payments has far-reaching implications. It could impact energy sector restructuring, economic sanctions, global influence, currency wars, and financial stability. As economists and politicians, it is our responsibility to thoroughly examine and understand these potential consequences to effectively navigate the changing dynamics of the global economy.

Objectives of the book

"The Dollar's Decline: How the Shift in Oil Payments Impacts the U.S. Economy" aims to provide economists and politicians with a comprehensive analysis of the potential consequences of the world's oil no longer being paid with U.S. dollars. This subchapter outlines the specific objectives of the book, which include:

1. Analyzing the effect of shifting oil payments on the value of the U.S. dollar and its position as a global reserve currency: This objective explores the potential impact on the U.S. dollar's value and its status as the dominant global currency when oil payments are denominated in other currencies. It delves into the repercussions for exchange rates and the U.S. economy's ability to maintain its currency's strength.

2. Examining the potential consequences on U.S. foreign relations and global power dynamics when oil is no longer paid in U.S. dollars: This objective investigates the geopolitical implications of a shift away from the U.S. dollar in oil payments. It explores how such a change could affect U.S. foreign relations, global influence, and power dynamics, considering the economic and political consequences.

3. Exploring how the shift away from oil payments in U.S. dollars could incentivize the U.S. to develop alternative energy sources and reduce dependence on oil: This objective focuses on energy independence and alternative fuels. It investigates how the changing oil payment landscape could motivate the U.S. to invest in alternative energy sources, reduce reliance on oil imports, and reshape the energy sector.

4. Investigating the impact on the U.S. trade balance and current account deficit when oil payments are no longer denominated in U.S. dollars: This objective analyzes the potential effects on the U.S. trade balance and current account deficit resulting from the shift in oil payment currencies. It examines the trade implications and the broader economic consequences on the U.S. balance of payments.

5. Analyzing the potential effects on inflation and consumer prices in the U.S. as a result of changing oil payment currencies: This objective delves into the potential impact on inflation and consumer prices in the U.S. It examines how changing oil payment currencies could influence domestic price levels and the overall inflationary environment.

These objectives provide a framework for understanding the multifaceted implications of the shift in oil payments away from the U.S. dollar. By addressing these key areas, the book aims to equip economists and policymakers with insights to navigate the potential challenges and opportunities that arise from this major economic shift.

Scope and limitations

The scope and limitations of the shift in oil payments from the U.S. dollar to other currencies have far-reaching implications for the U.S. economy, geopolitics, energy independence, trade balance, inflation, stock markets, monetary policy, energy sector restructuring, economic sanctions, and global influence. However, it is essential to understand the boundaries and challenges associated with this transition.

One major limitation is the impact on the value of the U.S. dollar and its position as a global reserve currency. As the demand for the U.S. dollar decreases, its value may depreciate, leading to higher import costs and inflationary pressures. This could affect the purchasing power of consumers and erode the dollar's dominance in international trade and finance.

Another limitation lies in the geopolitical implications of this shift. The United States' foreign relations and global power dynamics could be significantly affected. The reliance on the U.S. dollar for oil payments has given the U.S. considerable influence over international affairs. However, if oil payments are no longer denominated in dollars, it could weaken the U.S.'s ability to exert economic pressure and influence global events.

Furthermore, the shift in oil payment currencies could incentivize the U.S. to develop alternative energy sources and reduce dependence on oil. This may lead to an energy sector restructuring and changes in investment patterns. However, the transition to alternative energy sources is a complex process that requires substantial investments and technological advancements.

The impact on the U.S. trade balance and current account deficit is another crucial aspect. As oil payments are no longer denominated in U.S. dollars, it may affect the overall trade balance and potentially widen the current account deficit. This could have implications for the U.S. economy's stability and its ability to finance imports.

Additionally, changing oil payment currencies can have implications for the stock markets and investment flows. Investors may react to the uncertainty surrounding the shift, leading to market volatility and potential disruptions in capital flows. Moreover, the Federal Reserve's role in managing the U.S. economy during this transition is crucial. It must navigate the challenges associated with a changing global financial landscape and adjust its monetary policy accordingly.

Lastly, the use of alternative oil payment currencies could impact the effectiveness of U.S. economic sanctions and its global influence. If countries can bypass the U.S. dollar in oil transactions, it may undermine the efficacy of U.S. sanctions, limiting its ability to exert influence and control over international events.

Overall, the shift in oil payments from the U.S. dollar to other currencies has significant implications across various sectors. It is essential for economists and politicians to understand the scope and limitations of this transition and proactively address the challenges that arise from it. By doing so, they can effectively navigate the changing global economic landscape and minimize potential risks and instabilities.

Methodology

In this subchapter, we will explore the methodology used to analyze the various impacts of shifting oil payments away from the U.S. dollar. The research presented in this book aims to provide economists and politicians with a comprehensive understanding of the consequences that such a shift could have on the U.S. economy and global power dynamics.

To address the niches of this book, we employ a multi-faceted approach that includes quantitative analysis, economic modeling, and geopolitical analysis. By examining a range of factors, we can gain a holistic understanding of the potential implications of this significant change in the global oil market.

Our research begins by analyzing the impact on the value of the U.S. dollar. Through an in-depth examination of historical data and econometric modeling, we assess how shifting oil payments could affect the value of the U.S. dollar and its position as a global reserve currency. We consider factors such as exchange rates, international trade flows, and monetary policy to develop a comprehensive understanding of this complex relationship.

Next, we delve into the geopolitical implications of this shift. By considering the potential consequences on U.S. foreign relations and global power dynamics, we aim to provide policymakers with insights into how this change may reshape the international landscape. We analyze the potential impact on alliances, global influence, and the effectiveness of economic sanctions.

Furthermore, we explore the potential effects on energy independence and alternative fuels. By examining how the shift away from oil payments in U.S. dollars could incentivize the U.S. to develop alternative energy sources, we shed light on the potential opportunities and challenges in the energy sector. We consider how this shift may impact investment patterns and the restructuring of the U.S. energy sector.

Additionally, we investigate the impact on the U.S. trade balance and current account deficit. Through rigorous analysis of trade data and economic models, we provide insights into how changing oil payment currencies may affect the U.S. trade position and overall economic stability.

Finally, we consider the potential effects on inflation, consumer prices, stock markets, and investment flows. By examining historical data and conducting economic analysis, we aim to understand the potential consequences on these vital aspects of the U.S. economy.

Throughout this subchapter, we also examine the role of the Federal Reserve in managing the U.S. economy during this transition, as well as potential risks and challenges such as currency wars and financial instability.

By employing this comprehensive methodology, we offer a detailed analysis of the potential impacts of shifting oil payments away from the U.S. dollar. This research serves as a valuable resource for economists and politicians seeking to understand the potential consequences and make informed policy decisions in an evolving global economy.

Chapter 2: The Shift in Oil Payments

Historical overview of oil payments in U.S. dollars

The historical overview of oil payments in U.S. dollars is a crucial aspect in understanding the potential impacts of shifting oil payments to other currencies. For decades, the U.S. dollar has been the dominant currency used for international oil transactions. This arrangement, commonly referred to as the petrodollar system, has played a significant role in shaping the global economy and geopolitical dynamics.

The petrodollar system emerged in the early 1970s when the United States made agreements with Saudi Arabia, OPEC's largest oil producer, to price oil exclusively in U.S. dollars. This move had far-reaching implications for the U.S. economy, as it created a constant demand for dollars and strengthened its position as a global reserve currency. With oil being a vital commodity for every country, the petrodollar system effectively ensured the continuous demand for U.S. dollars, thereby increasing their value and maintaining the U.S. dollar's dominance in global trade.

The use of U.S. dollars for oil payments has not only provided economic benefits but has also exerted significant geopolitical influence. By controlling the currency used for oil transactions, the United States has been able to leverage its economic power to shape foreign relations and global power dynamics. It has allowed the U.S. to exert influence over oil-producing nations and maintain its position as a global superpower.

However, the historical overview also highlights the potential consequences when oil is no longer paid in U.S. dollars. As countries explore alternative currencies for oil payments, the value of the U.S. dollar may decline. The reduced demand for dollars could lead to a decrease in its value relative to other currencies, affecting its position as the dominant global reserve currency.

Moreover, the shift away from oil payments in U.S. dollars could incentivize the United States to develop alternative energy sources and reduce dependence on oil. This transition could have a significant impact on the U.S. energy sector and investment patterns, leading to a restructuring of the industry and potentially creating new opportunities for alternative fuels.

The implications of changing oil payment currencies extend beyond the economy. It could also have implications for U.S. foreign relations, global power dynamics, inflation, consumer prices, trade balance, and current account deficits. Additionally, the effectiveness of U.S. economic sanctions and its global influence may be affected by the use of alternative oil payment currencies.

As the world contemplates a shift away from the U.S. dollar as the dominant currency for oil payments, economists and politicians need to consider the potential risks and challenges. Currency wars and financial instability are among the key concerns that arise with such a transition. Understanding the historical context of oil payments in U.S. dollars is essential in comprehending the potential implications and formulating appropriate strategies to adapt to this changing landscape.

Factors driving the shift away from U.S. dollar payments

The global economic landscape is undergoing a profound transformation, with significant implications for the U.S. economy. One of the key drivers of this transformation is the shift away from U.S. dollar payments in the oil market. In this subchapter, we will explore the factors behind this shift and the potential consequences for various aspects of the U.S. economy.

Over the past decades, the U.S. dollar has enjoyed a dominant position as the currency of choice for oil payments. This arrangement has provided the U.S. with several economic advantages, such as increased demand for the dollar and the ability to finance its current account deficit through oil-related transactions. However, several factors are now challenging the dollar's status as the primary currency for oil payments.

Firstly, geopolitical dynamics are playing a crucial role in driving this shift. As countries seek to diversify their foreign exchange reserves and reduce their reliance on the U.S. dollar, they are exploring alternative payment currencies, such as the euro, the Chinese yuan, and even cryptocurrencies. This diversification is motivated by concerns over the U.S. dollar's dominance, as well as geopolitical tensions with the United States.

Secondly, the quest for energy independence and the development of alternative fuels is pushing countries away from oil payments in U.S. dollars. As nations prioritize renewable energy sources and reduce their dependence on oil, the need for oil payments denominated in U.S. dollars diminishes. This shift could incentivize the U.S. to accelerate its efforts in alternative energy development, which could have far-reaching implications for the energy sector and investment patterns.

The impact of this shift on the U.S. economy is multifaceted. On one hand, the value of the U.S. dollar could be negatively affected as demand for it decreases. This could lead to inflationary pressures and higher consumer prices, as the cost of imported goods rises. Additionally, the U.S. trade balance and current account deficit could be significantly impacted, as the country loses the economic benefits associated with oil payments in U.S. dollars.

Moreover, the shift away from the U.S. dollar as the dominant currency for oil payments could have geopolitical implications. The effectiveness of U.S. economic sanctions and its global influence may be compromised, as countries find alternative ways to circumvent these measures through the use of alternative payment currencies.

Furthermore, the role of the Federal Reserve in managing the U.S. economy will be crucial during this transition. The Federal Reserve will need to adapt its monetary policy to address the potential challenges arising from the shift away from the U.S. dollar as the primary currency for oil payments.

In conclusion, the factors driving the shift away from U.S. dollar payments in the oil market are complex and interrelated. The consequences for the U.S. economy are wide-ranging, including the potential impact on the value of the U.S. dollar, geopolitical dynamics, energy sector restructuring, and the effectiveness of economic sanctions. Understanding and preparing for these factors are of utmost importance for economists and politicians alike.

Implications of the shift for the U.S. economy

As the world begins to shift away from using the U.S. dollar for oil payments and adopts alternative currencies, the implications for the U.S. economy are far-reaching. This subchapter explores the various consequences and effects that this shift will have on the United States, focusing on key areas such as the U.S. dollar value, geopolitical implications, energy independence, trade balance, inflation, stock market, Federal Reserve, energy sector restructuring, economic sanctions, and currency wars.

One of the most significant implications is the impact on the U.S. dollar value and its position as a global reserve currency. With the reduced demand for U.S. dollars in international oil transactions, the value of the dollar is likely to decline. This can lead to higher import costs, inflationary pressures, and a decrease in the purchasing power of American consumers.

Geopolitically, the shift away from the U.S. dollar as the dominant currency for oil payments can have significant consequences on U.S. foreign relations and global power dynamics. The United States may experience a decrease in its influence and ability to leverage economic sanctions, as alternative payment currencies diminish the effectiveness of these measures.

However, this shift can also present an opportunity for the United States to prioritize energy independence and develop alternative fuel sources. With the incentive to reduce reliance on oil, the U.S. can invest in renewable energy technologies and decrease its carbon footprint. This transition can create new industries, generate jobs, and promote sustainable economic growth.

Furthermore, the change in oil payment currencies can impact the U.S. trade balance and current account deficit. As the demand for U.S. dollars decreases, the trade deficit may narrow, leading to a potential improvement in the overall balance of trade.

In terms of inflation and consumer prices, changing oil payment currencies can have varying effects. If alternative currencies are more stable than the U.S. dollar, inflationary pressures may be mitigated. However, if the shift leads to a decline in the dollar's value, imported goods may become more expensive, leading to higher consumer prices.

The shift away from the U.S. dollar can also have implications for the stock market and investment flows. Uncertainty and volatility may arise as investors reassess their portfolios and reallocate their investments. Additionally, the Federal Reserve will play a crucial role in managing the U.S. economy during this transition, ensuring stability and mitigating potential risks.

The energy sector is likely to undergo restructuring as the demand for oil payments in U.S. dollars diminishes. Investment patterns may change, with a shift towards renewable energy sources and away from traditional oil-related industries.

Lastly, the use of alternative oil payment currencies can impact the effectiveness of U.S. economic sanctions and its global influence. The United States may need to find alternative ways to exert its influence and maintain its position in global affairs.

Overall, the shift away from the U.S. dollar as the dominant currency for oil payments poses both challenges and opportunities for the U.S. economy. It is crucial for economists and politicians to understand and navigate these implications to ensure a smooth transition and long-term economic stability.

Chapter 3: Impact on the U.S. Dollar Value

Analyzing the effect of shifting oil payments on the value of the U.S. dollar

The global economy has long relied on the U.S. dollar as the dominant currency for oil payments. However, the landscape is rapidly changing, and the world is witnessing a shift away from the dollar as a result of various geopolitical and economic factors. This subchapter aims to analyze the effect of this shift on the value of the U.S. dollar, as well as its position as a global reserve currency.

The shift in oil payments away from the U.S. dollar can have significant consequences for the value of the currency. As countries begin to use alternative currencies for oil transactions, the demand for the dollar diminishes. This decrease in demand can lead to a depreciation of the dollar, potentially impacting its value against other major currencies. Economists and politicians need to closely monitor this shift and understand its implications for the U.S. economy.

Moreover, the use of alternative currencies for oil payments can also have geopolitical implications. The U.S. dollar has historically been a tool of American influence, as it gives the United States significant control over global financial transactions. If oil payments are denominated in other currencies, it could potentially diminish the U.S.'s global power and influence, as well as affect its foreign relations.

Additionally, the shift away from the dollar as the dominant currency for oil payments could incentivize the U.S. to develop alternative energy sources and reduce its dependence on oil. This transition could lead to the restructuring of the U.S. energy sector and investment patterns, as the country seeks to become more energy-independent.

Furthermore, the change in oil payment currencies can impact the U.S. trade balance and current account deficit. As the demand for the dollar decreases, it can affect the value of the currency, potentially leading to an increase in trade imbalances and a widening current account deficit.

Moreover, this shift can have implications for inflation and consumer prices in the U.S. The value of the dollar plays a crucial role in determining the cost of imports, including oil. If the value of the dollar depreciates, it could lead to higher import costs, potentially fueling inflation and impacting consumer prices.

In conclusion, the shift in oil payments away from the U.S. dollar can have far-reaching implications for the U.S. economy. It can impact the value of the dollar, its position as a global reserve currency, foreign relations, energy independence, trade balance, inflation, consumer prices, stock markets, investment flows, monetary policy, the energy sector, economic sanctions, global influence, and even pose risks of currency wars and financial instability. Economists and politicians need to carefully analyze and understand these effects to navigate the changing landscape of the global economy effectively.

The U.S. dollar as a global reserve currency

The U.S. dollar has long held the position of the global reserve currency, but what happens to the U.S. economy when the world's oil is no longer paid with U.S. dollars? This subchapter delves into the various implications of shifting oil payments away from the U.S. dollar and explores the potential consequences on the U.S. economy, geopolitics, energy independence, trade balance, inflation, stock markets, monetary policy, energy sector restructuring, economic sanctions, currency wars, and financial stability.

One of the key areas of concern is the impact on the value of the U.S. dollar and its position as a global reserve currency. Shifting oil payments to other currencies could lead to a depreciation of the dollar, potentially affecting its status as the international medium of exchange and store of value. This could have far-reaching effects on the U.S. economy, including increased costs of imports, reduced foreign investment, and changes in interest rates.

Geopolitically, the shift away from the U.S. dollar as the dominant currency for oil payments could have significant consequences for U.S. foreign relations and global power dynamics. It may alter the influence and leverage of the United States in international affairs, as well as impact the effectiveness of economic sanctions imposed by the U.S. on other countries.

The transition to alternative oil payment currencies may also incentivize the U.S. to develop alternative energy sources and reduce its dependence on oil. This could lead to a restructuring of the energy sector and changes in investment patterns, potentially driving innovation and promoting renewable energy technologies.

Furthermore, the shift away from the U.S. dollar could have implications for the U.S. trade balance and current account deficit. Changes in oil payment currencies may affect the demand for U.S. goods and services, potentially impacting export levels and overall trade dynamics.

In terms of inflation and consumer prices, changing oil payment currencies could influence the cost of oil imports and subsequently impact domestic inflation rates. This, in turn, would affect consumer prices and the purchasing power of individuals and businesses in the United States.

The subchapter also explores the potential consequences on U.S. stock markets and investment flows when the world's oil is no longer paid in U.S. dollars. Changes in oil payment currencies could lead to fluctuations in stock market performance and alter investment patterns, potentially impacting the overall stability of financial markets.

The role of the Federal Reserve in managing the U.S. economy during this transition is also analyzed. The Federal Reserve's monetary policy decisions may be influenced by the shift away from the U.S. dollar as the dominant oil payment currency, as it navigates the potential impact on inflation, interest rates, and overall economic stability.

Lastly, the subchapter investigates the potential risks and challenges posed by a shift away from the U.S. dollar as the dominant currency for oil payments. Currency wars and financial instability are examined, highlighting the potential risks associated with a loss of confidence in the U.S. dollar and the emergence of competing currencies.

In conclusion, the shift away from the U.S. dollar as the dominant currency for oil payments has far-reaching implications for the U.S. economy, geopolitics, energy sector, trade balance, inflation, stock markets, monetary policy, economic sanctions, currency wars, and financial stability. This subchapter provides a comprehensive analysis of these potential consequences, offering valuable insights for economists and politicians grappling with this complex issue.

Potential consequences for the U.S. economy

As the world's oil payments transition away from the U.S. dollar towards other currencies, there are several potential consequences for the U.S. economy that economists and politicians need to consider. These consequences range from the impact on the value of the U.S. dollar to geopolitical implications, energy independence, trade balance, inflation, stock markets, monetary policy, energy sector restructuring, economic sanctions, and financial instability.

One of the key concerns is the impact on the value of the U.S. dollar and its position as a global reserve currency. Shifting oil payments away from the dollar could lead to a decline in its value, as demand for the currency decreases. This could have far-reaching effects on the U.S. economy, including higher import costs, reduced purchasing power, and potential inflationary pressures.

Geopolitically, the shift away from the dollar as the currency for oil payments could have consequences on U.S. foreign relations and global power dynamics. The U.S. may lose some influence and leverage in international affairs, as the dollar's status as a dominant currency diminishes.

However, this transition could also incentivize the U.S. to develop alternative energy sources and reduce dependence on oil. With the loss of the dollar's monopoly in oil payments, the U.S. may be compelled to invest in renewable energy technologies and promote energy independence.

Furthermore, the change in oil payment currencies could have implications for the U.S. trade balance and current account deficit. If the dollar's demand decreases, it could lead to a decline in exports and an increase in imports, resulting in a larger trade deficit.

Inflation and consumer prices could also be affected by the shift in payment currencies. Changes in exchange rates and import costs could influence inflationary pressures and consumer prices, potentially impacting the purchasing power of American households.

The stock market and investment flows are not immune to these changes either. Shifting oil payment currencies could have consequences on U.S. stock markets and investment patterns. Investors may redirect their funds to economies that are now handling oil payments in alternative currencies, potentially impacting U.S. investment flows.

Additionally, the Federal Reserve will play a crucial role in managing the U.S. economy during this transition. Monetary policy adjustments may be necessary to mitigate any adverse effects on the U.S. dollar and the overall economy.

The energy sector itself may undergo restructuring as a result of the changing oil payment currencies. Investments in traditional oil extraction and exploration may decrease, while funds pour into alternative energy sources.

Moreover, the use of alternative oil payment currencies could impact the effectiveness of U.S. economic sanctions and its global influence. The ability to enforce economic restrictions and exert influence may weaken as the dollar's role diminishes.

Lastly, the shift away from the U.S. dollar as the dominant currency for oil payments could lead to currency wars and financial instability. As countries vie for dominance in the new payment system, conflicts may arise, potentially impacting global financial stability.

In conclusion, the shift in oil payments away from the U.S. dollar towards other currencies can have significant consequences for the U.S. economy. It is crucial for economists and politicians to thoroughly analyze and address these potential consequences to ensure a smooth transition and mitigate any negative impacts.

Chapter 4: Geopolitical Implications

Examining potential consequences on U.S. foreign relations

Examining potential consequences on U.S. foreign relations:

The global shift away from using the U.S. dollar as the dominant currency for oil payments has far-reaching implications for U.S. foreign relations. This subchapter delves into the potential consequences of this shift and its impact on the United States' global power dynamics.

One of the key consequences of moving away from the U.S. dollar as the primary currency for oil payments is the potential strain it may place on U.S. foreign relations. Historically, the U.S. dollar's status as the global reserve currency has given the United States significant influence and leverage in international affairs. However, as more countries opt to use alternative currencies for oil payments, the U.S. may find its influence waning.

This shift could also lead to a reconfiguration of global power dynamics. Countries that become key players in the new system of oil payments may gain increased political influence and leverage, potentially challenging U.S. dominance on the world stage. As the United States loses its privileged status as the sole provider of oil payment infrastructure, it may have to adapt its geopolitical strategies to maintain its influence.

Furthermore, the use of alternative currencies for oil payments may impact the effectiveness of U.S. economic sanctions. Currently, the U.S. has the ability to impose sanctions on countries by restricting their access to the U.S. dollar-based financial system. However, if countries can bypass the U.S. dollar for oil payments, they may also find ways to circumvent U.S. sanctions, reducing their impact and effectiveness.

Additionally, the shift away from the U.S. dollar as the dominant currency for oil payments could lead to currency wars and financial instability. As countries compete to establish their currencies as viable alternatives, there may be increased volatility in currency exchange rates. This volatility could create instability in global financial markets, which could have ripple effects on the U.S. economy.

Overall, the move away from the U.S. dollar as the primary currency for oil payments has significant implications for U.S. foreign relations. The United States may face challenges to its global influence, potential disruptions to its economic sanctions, and increased currency volatility. These consequences require careful consideration and strategic planning from economists and politicians as they navigate the evolving landscape of international relations and economic dynamics.

Global power dynamics and the shift in oil payments

The global power dynamics are set to undergo a significant shift as oil payments move away from being denominated in U.S. dollars to other currencies. This subchapter explores the various implications of this shift on the U.S. economy, geopolitical relations, energy independence, trade balance, inflation, stock markets, monetary policy, energy sector restructuring, economic sanctions, currency wars, and financial instability.

One of the primary concerns surrounding the shift in oil payments is the impact on the U.S. dollar value and its position as the global reserve currency. As oil payments become dominated by other currencies, the demand for the U.S. dollar may decrease, leading to a potential decline in its value. This could have far-reaching consequences for the U.S. economy and its standing in the global financial system.

Geopolitically, the shift in oil payments could have significant implications for U.S. foreign relations and global power dynamics. The reliance on the U.S. dollar for oil transactions has long provided the United States with a significant influence over global affairs. However, as other currencies gain prominence, the U.S. may lose some of its leverage and face challenges in maintaining its dominant position on the world stage.

The move away from U.S. dollar-denominated oil payments could also incentivize the U.S. to develop alternative energy sources and reduce its dependence on oil. This could have positive implications for energy independence and the environment, as the country looks for sustainable and renewable energy solutions.

Furthermore, the shift in oil payments could impact the U.S. trade balance and current account deficit. As the U.S. dollar loses its status as the primary currency for oil transactions, it may lead to a decrease in demand for the dollar in international trade, potentially affecting the trade balance and contributing to a higher current account deficit.

The transition to alternative oil payment currencies could also have implications for inflation and consumer prices in the U.S. The change in currency dynamics may affect the cost of imported oil and, in turn, impact the overall price levels in the economy, potentially leading to inflationary pressures.

Additionally, the shift in oil payments could have consequences for U.S. stock markets and investment flows. As the global oil trade diversifies its currency base, it may lead to changes in investment patterns, with potential implications for the performance of U.S. stock markets and the flow of capital into the country.

The Federal Reserve's role in managing the U.S. economy during this transition is also a crucial aspect to consider. The central bank may need to adjust its monetary policy to accommodate the changing dynamics of oil payments and the potential impact on the U.S. dollar and the broader economy.

The restructuring of the U.S. energy sector and investment patterns is another area of interest. With a shift away from oil payments in U.S. dollars, there may be a need for the United States to reevaluate its energy strategy and investment priorities, potentially leading to changes in the sector's landscape.

Moreover, the use of alternative oil payment currencies could impact the effectiveness of U.S. economic sanctions and its global influence. As countries opt to use other currencies for oil transactions, the efficacy of U.S. sanctions may be diminished, potentially reducing its ability to exercise influence on the global stage.

Lastly, the shift away from the U.S. dollar as the dominant currency for oil payments could lead to currency wars and financial instability. As countries compete to establish their currencies as alternatives, there may be increased volatility in currency markets and potential risks to global financial stability.

In conclusion, the shift in oil payments away from the U.S. dollar has far-reaching implications for economists and politicians. It affects the U.S. dollar value, geopolitical relations, energy independence, trade balance, inflation, stock markets, monetary policy, energy sector restructuring, economic sanctions, currency wars, and financial instability. Understanding and navigating these dynamics will be crucial for policymakers and economists in the coming years.

Chapter 5: Energy Independence and Alternative Fuels

Incentives for the U.S. to develop alternative energy sources

As the world gradually shifts away from using the U.S. dollar for oil payments and moves towards other currencies, it becomes crucial for the United States to explore alternative energy sources. This subchapter delves into the various incentives that the U.S. has to develop alternative energy sources and reduce its dependence on oil.

First and foremost, energy independence is a key incentive for the U.S. By developing alternative energy sources such as wind, solar, and nuclear power, the country can reduce its reliance on imported oil. This not only enhances national security but also reduces the vulnerability of the U.S. economy to fluctuations in global oil prices.

Furthermore, developing alternative energy sources would have a positive impact on the U.S. trade balance and current account deficit. Currently, the U.S. imports a significant amount of oil, which contributes to a substantial trade deficit. By transitioning towards alternative energy sources, the U.S. can reduce its oil imports, improving the trade balance and decreasing the current account deficit.

In addition, the development of alternative energy sources would lead to a significant reduction in greenhouse gas emissions, addressing environmental concerns. This would not only benefit the U.S. economy but also contribute to global efforts in combating climate change.

From an economic perspective, the development of alternative energy sources presents immense investment opportunities. As the world shifts away from oil payments in U.S. dollars, there will be a need for new infrastructure to support alternative energy production and distribution.

This will attract investment and stimulate economic growth, creating jobs and boosting the overall economy.

Moreover, the U.S. can enhance its global influence by becoming a leader in the renewable energy sector. By investing in research and development, the U.S. can develop cutting-edge technologies and export them to other countries, thus increasing its soft power and global standing.

Ultimately, the shift away from oil payments in U.S. dollars provides the U.S. with a unique opportunity to reshape its energy sector and reduce its dependence on oil. By embracing alternative energy sources, the U.S. can achieve energy independence, improve its trade balance, address environmental concerns, stimulate economic growth, and enhance its global influence. It is imperative for economists and politicians to recognize these incentives and take proactive measures to develop alternative energy sources for the benefit of the U.S. economy and its global position.

Reducing dependence on oil and its impact on the economy

As the global economy becomes increasingly interconnected, the reliance on oil as a key driver of economic growth has become a pressing concern for economists and politicians alike. This subchapter delves into the potential consequences of reducing dependence on oil and shifting away from using U.S. dollars as the primary currency for oil payments. By examining various aspects such as the impact on the U.S. dollar value, geopolitical implications, energy independence and alternative fuels, trade balance and current account deficit, inflation and consumer prices, stock market and investment implications, Federal Reserve and monetary policy, energy sector restructuring, economic sanctions and global influence, as well as currency wars and financial instability, this subchapter aims to provide a comprehensive analysis of the potential effects of such a shift.

One of the central issues explored in this subchapter is the impact on the U.S. dollar value and its position as a global reserve currency. Shifting oil payments away from the U.S. dollar could potentially undermine its value and erode its status as the dominant global currency. This, in turn, could have far-reaching consequences on the U.S. economy, including the potential for inflation and changes in consumer prices.

Additionally, the subchapter considers the geopolitical implications of such a shift. Examining the potential consequences on U.S. foreign relations and global power dynamics, it explores how the use of alternative oil payment currencies could impact the effectiveness of U.S. economic sanctions and its global influence.

Furthermore, this subchapter explores how reducing dependence on oil payments in U.S. dollars could incentivize the U.S. to develop alternative energy sources and reduce its overall dependence on oil. This could lead to a restructuring of the energy sector and changes in investment patterns, with potential implications for the stock market and investment flows.

The role of the Federal Reserve in managing the U.S. economy during this transition is also analyzed. By examining the potential impacts on monetary policy and the actions of the Federal Reserve, this subchapter seeks to shed light on how the U.S. economy could be managed in the face of changing oil payment currencies.

In conclusion, reducing dependence on oil and shifting away from U.S. dollars as the primary currency for oil payments poses numerous challenges and opportunities for the U.S. economy. By exploring various aspects such as the impact on the U.S. dollar value, geopolitical implications, energy independence, trade balance, inflation, stock market, Federal Reserve, energy sector restructuring, economic sanctions, and currency wars, this subchapter provides a comprehensive analysis of the potential consequences of such a shift. Economists and politicians will find this subchapter invaluable in understanding the complex dynamics at play and formulating informed policies for the future.

Chapter 6: Trade Balance and Current Account Deficit

Investigating the impact on the U.S. trade balance

The shift in oil payments from U.S. dollars to other currencies can have a significant impact on the U.S. trade balance and current account deficit. Traditionally, oil has been priced and traded in U.S. dollars, which has supported the currency's status as the dominant global reserve currency. However, as more countries move towards using alternative currencies for oil payments, the U.S. may face challenges in maintaining its trade balance.

One of the key implications of this shift is the potential for a decline in demand for U.S. dollars. As oil-exporting countries receive payments in other currencies, the demand for U.S. dollars will decrease. This can lead to a depreciation of the U.S. dollar, which in turn can make imports more expensive and exports more competitive. The result is a trade imbalance, with imports outweighing exports and contributing to a widening current account deficit.

Furthermore, the shift in oil payment currencies can also impact the competitiveness of U.S. industries. As the U.S. dollar depreciates, domestically produced goods become relatively cheaper for foreign buyers, boosting export demand. However, imports become more expensive, which can negatively affect industries reliant on imported inputs. This can lead to a decline in the competitiveness of these industries, potentially resulting in job losses and economic challenges.

It is important for policymakers to closely monitor and manage the impact of this shift on the U.S. trade balance. Measures such as promoting export-oriented industries, investing in research and development, and diversifying export markets can help mitigate the negative effects. Additionally, efforts to reduce the reliance on oil imports and develop alternative energy sources can also contribute to a more balanced trade position.

Overall, the shift in oil payment currencies away from the U.S. dollar poses both challenges and opportunities for the U.S. economy. While it may lead to a trade imbalance and current account deficit, it also presents an opportunity for the U.S. to reevaluate and strengthen its industries, promote energy independence, and explore alternative sources of growth. Policymakers and economists must carefully analyze and respond to these changes to ensure a sustainable and prosperous economic future for the United States.

The current account deficit and its relation to oil payments

The current account deficit refers to the difference between a country's total exports and imports of goods, services, and transfers. It is an important indicator of a nation's economic health and can have significant implications for its currency, trade balance, and overall economic stability. In the context of oil payments, the current account deficit takes on even greater significance.

Traditionally, the world's oil payments have been predominantly denominated in U.S. dollars. This has given the United States certain advantages, such as increased demand for its currency and the ability to finance its current account deficit through the inflow of petrodollars. However, as the global economy evolves and new economic powers emerge, there is a growing possibility that oil payments may no longer be made in U.S. dollars but in other currencies.

This shift in oil payments could have several implications for the U.S. economy. Firstly, it would impact the value of the U.S. dollar. With a reduced demand for dollars, its value could decline, leading to higher import prices and potentially increasing inflationary pressures.

Additionally, the U.S. dollar's position as the global reserve currency could be undermined, as other currencies gain prominence in international trade.

The change in oil payment currencies could also have geopolitical implications. The U.S. has historically used the dominance of the U.S. dollar in oil payments to exert influence over global power dynamics and foreign relations. If other currencies take over this role, it could potentially weaken the U.S.'s global standing and limit its ability to enforce economic sanctions.

On the other hand, this shift could also incentivize the U.S. to develop alternative energy sources and reduce its dependence on oil. With oil payments no longer tied to the U.S. dollar, there may be increased motivation to explore renewable energy options and enhance energy independence. This could lead to significant changes in the U.S. energy sector and investment patterns.

Furthermore, the shift away from the U.S. dollar as the dominant currency for oil payments could have implications for the U.S. trade balance and current account deficit. A decline in demand for dollars could impact the U.S.'s ability to finance its deficit, potentially leading to a worsening trade balance.

Overall, the transition to alternative oil payment currencies could have far-reaching consequences for the U.S. economy, including its currency value, trade balance, energy sector, and geopolitical influence. Understanding these implications is crucial for economists and politicians alike as they navigate the changing dynamics of the global economy and adapt to new challenges and opportunities.

Chapter 7: Inflation and Consumer Prices

Analyzing potential effects on inflation in the U.S.

Inflation is a key concern for economists and policymakers as it directly impacts the purchasing power of consumers and the stability of the economy. The subchapter on analyzing potential effects on inflation in the U.S. aims to explore the consequences of shifting oil payments from U.S. dollars to other currencies.

One of the primary concerns regarding inflation is the impact on consumer prices. When oil payments are no longer denominated in U.S. dollars, it can lead to increased costs for importing oil, which in turn can drive up prices for gasoline, transportation, and other goods and services dependent on oil. This can have a cascading effect on the overall inflation rate, potentially leading to higher prices across the economy.

Furthermore, the shift in oil payment currencies can also affect the value of the U.S. dollar. As the demand for U.S. dollars decreases in international oil transactions, the value of the dollar may depreciate. A weaker dollar can contribute to higher import prices, further fueling inflationary pressures.

Additionally, the Federal Reserve plays a crucial role in managing inflation through monetary policy. With the transition to alternative oil payment currencies, the Federal Reserve may need to adjust its policies to account for potential changes in inflation dynamics. This could involve implementing tighter monetary measures to counteract inflationary pressures or adopting a more accommodative stance to spur economic growth.

Moreover, the impact on inflation in the U.S. economy can have broader implications for the stock market and investment flows. Rising inflation erodes the real value of investment returns and can lead to increased market volatility. Investors may seek alternative assets or markets that offer better protection against inflation, potentially diverting capital away from U.S. stock markets.

Lastly, the potential risks and challenges associated with a shift away from the U.S. dollar as the dominant currency for oil payments can lead to currency wars and financial instability. As countries compete to establish their currencies as alternatives to the dollar, exchange rate fluctuations and currency devaluations can disrupt global trade and investment patterns, further exacerbating inflationary pressures.

In conclusion, the subchapter on analyzing potential effects on inflation in the U.S. highlights the importance of understanding how shifting oil payment currencies can impact inflation, consumer prices, the value of the U.S. dollar, monetary policy, stock markets, and global financial stability. Economists and policymakers must carefully evaluate these potential effects to develop appropriate strategies and policies to mitigate any adverse consequences on the U.S. economy.

Impact on consumer prices and purchasing power

In this subchapter, we will explore the impact on consumer prices and purchasing power resulting from the shift in oil payments away from the U.S. dollar. This shift has far-reaching implications for economists and politicians, as it will fundamentally alter the dynamics of the U.S. economy.

One of the key concerns surrounding this shift is the potential effect on consumer prices. As oil prices are denominated in other currencies, the value of the U.S. dollar may weaken, leading to inflationary pressures. This could lead to an increase in the prices of goods and services, reducing consumers' purchasing power. Economists and politicians must carefully consider the potential consequences of this shift on the average American's ability to afford basic necessities and discretionary spending.

Furthermore, the shift in oil payments could also impact the U.S. trade balance and current account deficit. Traditionally, oil payments in U.S. dollars have helped support the demand for the currency, allowing the U.S. to import goods and services from other countries. However, if oil payments are no longer denominated in U.S. dollars, this could lead to a reduction in the demand for the currency, potentially widening the trade deficit.

Another important consideration is the potential impact on the stock market and investment flows. The U.S. dollar has long been considered a safe haven currency, attracting global investors. However, if the U.S. dollar loses its position as the dominant currency for oil payments, this could lead to a decline in investor confidence and a shift in investment patterns. Economists and politicians must carefully evaluate the potential consequences on the stock market and overall investment climate.

Additionally, the Federal Reserve's role in managing the U.S. economy during this transition is crucial. The central bank will need to carefully monitor the impact of changing oil payment currencies on inflation, consumer prices, and overall economic stability. Monetary policies may need to be adjusted to mitigate any potential risks and ensure a smooth transition.

Lastly, this shift in oil payments could have geopolitical implications, impacting U.S. foreign relations and global power dynamics. The use of alternative oil payment currencies may weaken the effectiveness of U.S. economic sanctions and reduce the country's global influence. This could have significant consequences for the U.S. in terms of maintaining its geopolitical standing and exerting influence on the world stage.

In conclusion, the shift in oil payments away from the U.S. dollar will have profound effects on consumer prices and purchasing power, trade balances, stock markets, monetary policy, and global power dynamics.

Economists and politicians must carefully analyze and address these implications to ensure the stability and prosperity of the U.S. economy in a changing global landscape.

Chapter 8: Stock Market and Investment Implications

Examining potential consequences for U.S. stock markets

The shift in oil payments away from the U.S. dollar towards other currencies raises significant concerns for economists and politicians, particularly when it comes to the potential consequences for U.S. stock markets. This subchapter delves into the various implications that such a shift could have on the stability and performance of the U.S. stock market, as well as the broader implications for investment flows and market dynamics.

One immediate consequence of the shift in oil payments is the effect on the value of the U.S. dollar. As oil is currently priced in U.S. dollars, any move away from this arrangement could weaken the dollar's position as a global reserve currency. This, in turn, could lead to a depreciation in the value of the dollar, making U.S. stocks less attractive to foreign investors.

Furthermore, the potential for a weaker dollar could also impact inflation and consumer prices. If the dollar depreciates, imported goods, including oil, could become more expensive, leading to higher inflation and increased consumer prices. This could have a negative impact on consumer spending and, consequently, on the performance of U.S. companies listed on the stock market.

Additionally, the shift in oil payment currencies could also have geopolitical implications. The United States, as the dominant currency for oil payments, has enjoyed significant geopolitical influence. However, if oil payments are denominated in other currencies, it could potentially diminish the influence and power of the United States on the global stage. This could have a ripple effect on U.S. stock markets, as investors may perceive a decline in the stability and strength of the U.S. economy.

Another consequence to consider is the impact on the energy sector and investment patterns. Shifting away from oil payments in U.S. dollars could incentivize the United States to develop alternative energy sources and reduce dependence on oil. This could lead to a restructuring of the energy sector and a redirection of investment flows towards renewable energy and other sustainable industries. These changes could reshape the composition of the stock market, with potential winners and losers emerging.

Moreover, the role of the Federal Reserve in managing the U.S. economy during this transition cannot be overlooked. The Federal Reserve may need to implement new monetary policies to mitigate the potential disruptions caused by the shift in oil payment currencies. This could have implications for interest rates, liquidity, and overall market stability, all of which could impact stock market performance.

In conclusion, the shift in oil payments away from the U.S. dollar towards other currencies raises a myriad of potential consequences for U.S. stock markets. From the impact on the value of the U.S. dollar and potential inflationary pressures to geopolitical implications and the restructuring of the energy sector, economists and politicians must carefully examine and navigate these potential risks and opportunities to ensure the stability and long-term growth of the U.S. stock market.

Investment flows and their relation to changing oil payment currencies

The global oil market has long operated under the dominance of the U.S. dollar as the primary currency for oil payments. However, as the world moves towards a shift in oil payment currencies, economists and politicians are increasingly interested in understanding the implications of this change on investment flows and its impact on the U.S. economy.

The shift away from the U.S. dollar as the dominant currency for oil payments is likely to have significant implications for investment flows.

As oil-exporting countries start accepting alternative currencies for their oil, investors will need to adjust their portfolios to reflect this new reality. This adjustment could lead to a reallocation of investments away from the U.S. dollar and towards the currencies of countries that are now accepting oil payments in their own currency.

One potential consequence of this reallocation is a decline in demand for U.S. dollar-denominated assets, such as U.S. Treasury bonds. This could put downward pressure on the value of the U.S. dollar and have implications for the U.S. economy. A weaker U.S. dollar could make imports more expensive, leading to higher inflation and potentially impacting consumer prices.

Furthermore, the changing oil payment currencies could also impact the U.S. stock markets and investment patterns. As investors reallocate their portfolios, they may seek opportunities in countries that are now accepting alternative currencies for oil payments. This could result in increased investment in these countries' stock markets and potentially lead to a shift in global investment patterns.

The Federal Reserve will also play a crucial role in managing the U.S. economy during this transition. As the value of the U.S. dollar fluctuates, the Federal Reserve may need to adjust monetary policy to maintain stability. This could include actions such as interest rate changes or implementing quantitative easing measures to support the U.S. economy.

Moreover, the shift in oil payment currencies could have geopolitical implications. Countries that are no longer dependent on the U.S. dollar for oil payments may have greater flexibility in their foreign relations and global power dynamics. The effectiveness of U.S. economic sanctions could also be impacted as the use of alternative oil payment currencies may undermine their effectiveness.

In conclusion, the shift in oil payment currencies away from the U.S. dollar will have far-reaching implications for investment flows and the U.S. economy. It is crucial for economists and politicians to closely analyze the potential consequences on the value of the U.S. dollar, investment patterns, trade balance, inflation, and the role of the Federal Reserve. Additionally, the geopolitical implications, energy sector restructuring, and risks such as currency wars and financial instability should be carefully considered. Understanding these dynamics will be essential for policymakers in managing the transition to alternative oil payment currencies and ensuring the stability and prosperity of the U.S. economy.

Chapter 9: Federal Reserve and Monetary Policy

The role of the Federal Reserve during the transition

As the world shifts away from using the U.S. dollar as the primary currency for oil payments, the role of the Federal Reserve becomes crucial in managing the U.S. economy during this transition. The Federal Reserve, often referred to as the central bank of the United States, has the responsibility of maintaining price stability, promoting full employment, and ensuring the stability of the financial system.

One of the key challenges the Federal Reserve faces during this transition is managing the impact on the value of the U.S. dollar and its position as a global reserve currency. As oil payments are denominated in other currencies, there is a risk that the demand for the U.S. dollar may decline, potentially leading to a depreciation in its value. The Federal Reserve must employ appropriate monetary policy tools to prevent excessive volatility in the currency markets and maintain confidence in the U.S. dollar.

Furthermore, the Federal Reserve must closely monitor the potential consequences on U.S. foreign relations and global power dynamics. As the U.S. dollar loses its dominant role in oil payments, there may be geopolitical implications that could affect the United States' influence and relationships with other countries. The Federal Reserve must work with policymakers and economists to understand and manage these implications effectively.

The shift away from oil payments in U.S. dollars could also incentivize the U.S. to develop alternative energy sources and reduce dependence on oil. The Federal Reserve must support and facilitate this transition by providing necessary financial resources and implementing policies that encourage investment in the development of alternative fuels. Additionally, the Federal Reserve should collaborate with other government agencies and international organizations to promote sustainable energy practices and reduce the overall impact on the environment.

The impact on the U.S. trade balance and current account deficit is another area the Federal Reserve must carefully monitor. With the change in oil payment currencies, there could be fluctuations in the trade balance and the current account deficit. The Federal Reserve must employ appropriate monetary policy tools to ensure a stable and balanced trade environment and avoid any adverse effects on the U.S. economy.

Inflation and consumer prices are also areas of concern during this transition. The Federal Reserve must analyze and anticipate the potential effects of changing oil payment currencies on inflation and consumer prices. They must implement effective monetary policy measures to manage any potential inflationary pressures and ensure that consumer prices remain stable.

The Federal Reserve's role in managing the U.S. economy during the transition extends to the stock market and investment implications as well. The shift away from the U.S. dollar as the dominant currency for oil payments could have consequences on U.S. stock markets and investment flows. The Federal Reserve must work closely with financial institutions and market participants to mitigate any potential disruptions and maintain stability in the financial markets.

Lastly, the Federal Reserve needs to assess the potential risks and challenges posed by a shift away from the U.S. dollar as the dominant currency for oil payments. Currency wars and financial instability are significant concerns that the Federal Reserve must address. They must collaborate with other central banks and international organizations to mitigate these risks and maintain global financial stability.

Overall, the Federal Reserve plays a critical role in managing the U.S. economy during the transition to alternative oil payment currencies. They must carefully monitor and address the impact on the U.S. dollar value, foreign relations, trade balance, inflation, consumer prices, stock markets, and investment flows. By implementing appropriate monetary policy measures and collaborating with relevant stakeholders, the Federal Reserve can help ensure a smooth and successful transition while maintaining economic stability and global influence.

Managing the U.S. economy amidst changing oil payment currencies

In today's interconnected global economy, the U.S. dollar plays a central role as the dominant currency for oil payments. However, the world is witnessing a significant shift in this paradigm, with the potential for oil payments to be denominated in currencies other than the U.S. dollar. This subchapter aims to explore the various dimensions and implications of this shift, focusing on its impact on the U.S. economy.

One of the key areas of concern is the impact on the value of the U.S. dollar and its position as a global reserve currency. By analyzing the effect of shifting oil payments on the value of the dollar, economists and politicians can better understand the potential consequences for the U.S. economy. This includes examining the potential geopolitical implications, as the U.S. dollar's role as the dominant currency has historically given the United States significant leverage in foreign relations and global power dynamics.

Furthermore, the shift away from oil payments in U.S. dollars could incentivize the United States to develop alternative energy sources and reduce its dependence on oil. This exploration of energy independence and alternative fuels is crucial in understanding how the U.S. economy can adapt and thrive in a changing landscape.

An investigation into the impact on the U.S. trade balance and current account deficit when oil payments are no longer denominated in U.S. dollars is also vital. Understanding the potential consequences on inflation and consumer prices as a result of changing oil payment currencies is crucial for policymakers and economists alike.

Moreover, the potential consequences on U.S. stock markets and investment flows when the world's oil is no longer paid in U.S. dollars must be examined. This analysis can shed light on the potential risks and opportunities for investors and the broader economy.

The role of the Federal Reserve in managing the U.S. economy during the transition to alternative oil payment currencies is of utmost importance. Analyzing the Federal Reserve's role in monetary policy during this period can provide insights into how the U.S. can navigate potential economic challenges.

Exploring the potential changes in the U.S. energy sector and investment patterns resulting from shifting oil payment currencies is also essential. This examination can provide valuable insights into the restructuring of the energy sector and the potential opportunities for investment.

Lastly, investigating how the use of alternative oil payment currencies could impact the effectiveness of U.S. economic sanctions and its global influence is crucial. Evaluating the potential risks and challenges, including currency wars and financial instability, is essential for policymakers.

In conclusion, managing the U.S. economy amidst changing oil payment currencies requires a comprehensive understanding of the various dimensions and implications. This subchapter aims to provide economists and politicians with valuable insights into these areas of concern, enabling them to make informed decisions and policies for the future.

Chapter 10: Energy Sector Restructuring

Potential changes in the U.S. energy sector

The U.S. energy sector is poised for significant changes as the world shifts away from using the U.S. dollar as the dominant currency for oil payments. This subchapter explores the potential implications of this shift on various aspects of the U.S. economy, specifically focusing on the energy sector.

One of the most significant changes that could occur is the increased incentive for the U.S. to develop alternative energy sources and reduce its dependence on oil. With the decline in the dollar's role in oil payments, the U.S. may see the need to invest in renewable energy technologies and promote energy independence. This could lead to a restructuring of the U.S. energy sector, with a greater emphasis on clean energy solutions.

Additionally, the shift in oil payment currencies could have implications for the U.S. trade balance and current account deficit. As oil payments are no longer denominated in U.S. dollars, the U.S. may experience a decrease in demand for the currency, potentially impacting its value. This could lead to changes in the U.S. stock markets and investment flows, as investors reassess the attractiveness of dollar-denominated assets.

Furthermore, the use of alternative oil payment currencies could have geopolitical implications for the U.S. and its global power dynamics. It may impact U.S. foreign relations and the effectiveness of economic sanctions, as the use of alternative currencies could undermine the U.S.'s influence and ability to enforce its policies.

The Federal Reserve and monetary policy would also play a crucial role in managing the U.S. economy during the transition to alternative oil payment currencies. The Federal Reserve would need to navigate the changing dynamics and potential financial instability that could arise from a shift away from the U.S. dollar as the dominant currency.

Moreover, the shift in oil payment currencies may have an impact on inflation and consumer prices in the U.S. as well. Changes in the value of the U.S. dollar could affect the cost of imported goods, including oil, and subsequently influence overall inflation levels and consumer purchasing power.

Overall, the potential changes in the U.S. energy sector resulting from shifting oil payment currencies are wide-ranging and complex. Economists and politicians must carefully analyze the implications on energy independence, trade balances, inflation, stock markets, and global influence to effectively navigate this transition and ensure the continued stability and growth of the U.S. economy.

Investment patterns resulting from shifting oil payment currencies

As the world's oil payments gradually shift away from the U.S. dollar towards other currencies, economists and politicians are closely examining the potential investment patterns that may emerge. This subchapter delves into the various implications and consequences of this shift, shedding light on the influence it could have on the global economy, financial markets, and geopolitical dynamics.

One of the key areas of concern is the impact on the U.S. dollar's value and its position as a global reserve currency. With oil no longer being paid for in U.S. dollars, the demand for the currency may decline, leading to a potential depreciation. This depreciation could have far-reaching effects on the U.S. economy, including inflation and consumer prices, as well as the trade balance and current account deficit.

Furthermore, the shift in oil payment currencies could have significant geopolitical implications. It may alter the dynamics of U.S. foreign relations and global power structures, as the influence of the U.S. wanes with the diminishing importance of the U.S. dollar in international transactions. This shift could also impact the effectiveness of U.S. economic sanctions, as alternative payment currencies may undermine the ability to exert financial pressure on targeted countries.

The transition to alternative oil payment currencies could also incentivize the U.S. to develop alternative energy sources and reduce dependence on oil. With the potential decline in the value and importance of oil, the U.S. may seek to invest more heavily in renewable energy and other forms of energy production. This restructuring of the energy sector could lead to significant changes in investment patterns, with increased focus on green technologies and sustainable energy solutions.

Moreover, the shift away from the U.S. dollar as the dominant currency for oil payments could have implications for the stock market and investment flows. Investors may reevaluate their portfolios and seek alternative assets as the global financial landscape undergoes changes. This shift could create new investment opportunities and potential risks as markets adjust to the new reality.

To navigate these changes, the role of the Federal Reserve in managing the U.S. economy becomes crucial. The Federal Reserve will need to carefully consider the impact of alternative oil payment currencies on monetary policy and economic stability. This includes monitoring inflationary pressures and adjusting interest rates accordingly.

In conclusion, the shift in oil payment currencies has significant implications for investment patterns and the global economy. The impact on the U.S. dollar's value, geopolitical dynamics, energy independence, trade balance, inflation, and investment flows all require careful analysis and consideration. As economists and politicians delve into these topics, it becomes clear that the transition to alternative oil payment currencies will reshape investment patterns and have far-reaching consequences for the U.S. economy and its position in the world.

Chapter 11: Economic Sanctions and Global Influence

Impact on the effectiveness of U.S. economic sanctions

As the world transitions away from using the U.S. dollar as the dominant currency for oil payments, there are significant implications for the effectiveness of U.S. economic sanctions. Historically, the United States has relied on its position as the issuer of the world's reserve currency to enforce economic sanctions against countries that violate international norms or pose a threat to U.S. interests. However, as oil payments shift to other currencies, the ability of the U.S. to leverage economic sanctions may be diminished.

One of the main challenges with the shift away from the U.S. dollar is that it reduces the influence and reach of U.S. financial institutions. These institutions have traditionally played a crucial role in enforcing economic sanctions by blocking access to the U.S. financial system for sanctioned individuals, entities, or countries. With the decline in the use of the U.S. dollar, other countries and financial centers could step in, allowing sanctioned parties to bypass U.S. sanctions and continue their activities.

Moreover, the use of alternative oil payment currencies could also lead to the creation of alternative international payment systems that are less susceptible to U.S. control. This could make it more difficult for the U.S. to monitor and enforce economic sanctions effectively. Countries that are subject to U.S. sanctions may seek to establish alternative financial mechanisms to facilitate trade and financial transactions, further undermining the impact of U.S. economic sanctions.

Additionally, the shift away from the U.S. dollar as the dominant currency for oil payments could impact the willingness of other countries to comply with U.S. sanctions. As the U.S. loses its economic dominance, it may be seen as less influential and its sanctions may carry less weight. This could lead to a decrease in the effectiveness of U.S. economic sanctions, as countries may be more willing to defy or circumvent them.

In conclusion, the shift away from the U.S. dollar as the dominant currency for oil payments has significant implications for the effectiveness of U.S. economic sanctions. The reduced influence of U.S. financial institutions, the creation of alternative payment systems, and the decreased willingness of other countries to comply with U.S. sanctions could all contribute to a decline in the effectiveness of U.S. economic sanctions. This has important implications for both the U.S. economy and its global influence, and policymakers and economists must carefully consider these factors when evaluating the future of U.S. economic sanctions.

The influence of alternative oil payment currencies on global dynamics

In recent years, there has been growing speculation about the potential shift away from the U.S. dollar as the dominant currency for oil payments. This subchapter aims to explore the various implications of such a shift on global dynamics, with a particular focus on its impact on the U.S. economy. Economists and politicians alike must understand the potential consequences of this shift in order to prepare for the changes that lie ahead.

One of the key areas of concern is the impact on the U.S. dollar value and its position as a global reserve currency. As oil payments no longer rely on the dollar, its value may depreciate, leading to inflation and higher consumer prices. This could have far-reaching effects on the U.S. economy, including a potential decline in the stock market and changes in investment flows. Moreover, the Federal Reserve will need to carefully manage monetary policy during this transition to maintain stability.

The shift away from the U.S. dollar as the primary oil payment currency also has geopolitical implications. It could lead to changes in U.S. foreign relations and global power dynamics. As countries diversify their currency holdings, it may weaken the influence of the United States and its ability to impose economic sanctions effectively. This, in turn, could impact the country's global influence.

Furthermore, the move away from the U.S. dollar could incentivize the United States to develop alternative energy sources and reduce its dependence on oil. With the decline in oil payments, the country may be prompted to invest in renewable energy technologies, thereby advancing energy independence and reducing the environmental impact of fossil fuels.

An important consideration is the impact on the U.S. trade balance and current account deficit. As oil payments are denominated in currencies other than the U.S. dollar, it may affect the nation's trade balance and potentially widen the current account deficit. This could have consequences for the overall stability of the U.S. economy.

Additionally, the restructuring of the energy sector will be a significant outcome. Shifting oil payment currencies will likely result in changes in investment patterns within the U.S. energy sector. This may lead to a reallocation of resources and a transformation of the sector, potentially affecting job markets and regional economies.

Lastly, one must not overlook the potential risks and challenges associated with a shift away from the U.S. dollar. Currency wars and financial instability are possible outcomes, as countries compete to establish their currencies as viable alternatives for oil payments. Such instability could have ripple effects throughout the global financial system.

In conclusion, the influence of alternative oil payment currencies on global dynamics is a complex and multifaceted issue. It holds significant implications for economists and politicians, impacting various aspects of the U.S. economy and its global standing. Understanding these implications is crucial for effectively managing the transition and ensuring long-term stability and prosperity.

Chapter 12: Currency Wars and Financial Instability

Risks and challenges posed by a shift away from the U.S. dollar

As the global economy evolves, there is a growing possibility of a significant shift away from the U.S. dollar as the dominant currency for oil payments. This shift would have wide-ranging implications for the U.S. economy, geopolitics, energy independence, trade balance, inflation, stock markets, monetary policy, energy sector restructuring, economic sanctions, and global influence.

One of the major risks and challenges associated with this shift is the impact on the value of the U.S. dollar and its position as a global reserve currency. If oil payments are denominated in other currencies, it could lead to a decline in demand for the dollar, resulting in a depreciation of its value. This would have implications for the purchasing power of the dollar, as well as the ability of the U.S. to finance its current account deficit.

Geopolitically, the shift away from the U.S. dollar could have consequences for U.S. foreign relations and global power dynamics. The dollar's status as the dominant currency has provided the U.S. with significant influence in international affairs. If oil payments are no longer made in dollars, it could weaken the U.S.'s economic leverage and alter the balance of power among nations.

However, this shift could also incentivize the U.S. to develop alternative energy sources and reduce its dependence on oil. With the need to secure stable energy supplies, the U.S. may invest more in renewable energy and other sustainable solutions. This could lead to a restructuring of the energy sector and new investment patterns, creating opportunities for economic growth and job creation.

On the trade front, a shift away from the U.S. dollar in oil payments could impact the U.S. trade balance and current account deficit. The reduced demand for dollars could result in a decrease in exports and an increase in imports, leading to trade imbalances. This could have implications for domestic industries, employment, and overall economic stability.

Furthermore, the shift away from the U.S. dollar could have effects on inflation and consumer prices in the U.S. If the dollar depreciates, it could lead to higher import prices, including the cost of oil. This could put upward pressure on inflation, affecting the purchasing power of consumers and potentially impacting economic growth.

In terms of financial markets, a shift away from the U.S. dollar as the dominant currency for oil payments could have consequences for stock markets and investment flows. Investors may adjust their portfolios and reallocate funds away from U.S. assets, leading to volatility in financial markets. Additionally, the Federal Reserve would face challenges in managing monetary policy during this transition, as it would need to balance the impact on the economy and financial stability.

Moreover, the use of alternative oil payment currencies could impact the effectiveness of U.S. economic sanctions and its global influence. If countries choose to use alternate currencies, it could undermine the effectiveness of U.S. sanctions, reducing the U.S.'s ability to influence global events and exert economic pressure.

Lastly, the shift away from the U.S. dollar could also lead to currency wars and financial instability. As countries compete for dominance in the new oil payment landscape, there could be increased volatility in currency markets and potential conflicts over exchange rates. This could pose risks to global financial stability and create uncertainties for businesses and investors.

In conclusion, the risks and challenges posed by a shift away from the U.S. dollar as the dominant currency for oil payments are significant and wide-ranging. From the value of the dollar to geopolitical implications, energy sector restructuring to inflation, and financial instability, economists and politicians must carefully analyze and address these potential risks and challenges to navigate the changing global economic landscape.

Potential outcomes including currency wars and financial instability

Currency wars and financial instability are potential outcomes that may arise from a shift away from the U.S. dollar as the dominant currency for oil payments. This subchapter will explore the risks and challenges associated with this transition and the implications for economists and politicians.

One of the major concerns is the possibility of currency wars. As countries start to use alternative currencies for oil payments, there may be a race to devalue their own currencies to gain a competitive advantage in the global market. This can lead to a vicious cycle of currency devaluations, making it difficult for countries to maintain stable exchange rates. Economists and politicians need to carefully monitor and manage these currency dynamics to avoid a destabilizing currency war.

Financial instability is another potential outcome. The U.S. dollar has long been considered a safe haven currency, with many countries holding large reserves of dollars. If the demand for dollars decreases as a result of the shift in oil payments, it could lead to a depreciation of the dollar. This can have a ripple effect on global financial markets, causing volatility and uncertainty. Policymakers will need to implement measures to ensure financial stability during this transition period.

The subchapter will also examine the potential impact on global power dynamics and U.S. foreign relations. The U.S. dollar's status as the world's reserve currency has given the United States significant influence over global economic and political affairs. If the dollar's dominance is diminished, it could weaken the U.S.'s position on the global stage, affecting its ability to exert influence and negotiate favorable trade deals.

Furthermore, the shift away from oil payments in U.S. dollars could have implications for energy independence and alternative fuels. With reduced dependence on oil, the U.S. may be incentivized to develop alternative energy sources, such as renewables, which could have positive environmental and economic impacts.

The subchapter will also explore the impact on the U.S. trade balance and current account deficit. As oil payments are denominated in alternative currencies, there may be fluctuations in the trade balance, potentially affecting the overall health of the U.S. economy.

Additionally, economists and politicians will need to analyze the potential effects on inflation and consumer prices resulting from changing oil payment currencies. Fluctuations in currency values can impact import and export prices, potentially leading to inflationary pressures or changes in consumer purchasing power.

The implications for the stock market and investment flows will also be examined. A shift away from the U.S. dollar as the dominant currency for oil payments could lead to changes in investment patterns and investor sentiment, potentially impacting the performance of U.S. stock markets.

The role of the Federal Reserve in managing the U.S. economy during this transition will also be analyzed. As the central bank, the Federal Reserve will need to adjust monetary policy to adapt to the changing currency dynamics and mitigate any potential risks to the U.S. economy.

The subchapter will also discuss potential changes in the U.S. energy sector and investment patterns resulting from shifting oil payment currencies. With the reduced reliance on oil, there may be a restructuring of the energy sector, with increased investments in alternative energy sources.

Lastly, the subchapter will explore how the use of alternative oil payment currencies could impact the effectiveness of U.S. economic sanctions and its global influence. If countries can bypass the U.S. dollar for oil payments, it may undermine the efficacy of economic sanctions imposed by the U.S., potentially reducing its global influence.

Overall, this subchapter will provide economists and politicians with a comprehensive analysis of the potential risks and challenges associated with a shift away from the U.S. dollar as the dominant currency for oil payments. It will explore the implications for various aspects of the U.S. economy and global dynamics, highlighting the need for careful management and policy considerations during this transition.

Chapter 13: Conclusion

Summary of key findings

In "The Dollar's Decline: How the Shift in Oil Payments Impacts the U.S. Economy," we delve into the consequences of a significant shift away from using U.S. dollars as the primary currency for oil payments. This subchapter aims to provide a concise summary of the key findings explored throughout the book, targeting economists and politicians interested in understanding the potential implications of this shift on various aspects of the U.S. cconomy.

We begin by analyzing the impact on the value of the U.S. dollar and its position as a global reserve currency. The findings suggest that the shift in oil payments could potentially weaken the U.S. dollar, leading to a decline in its global dominance and altering the dynamics of the international monetary system.

Examining the geopolitical implications, we discover that a move away from U.S. dollar-denominated oil payments could have far-reaching consequences on U.S. foreign relations and global power dynamics. It may lead to shifts in alliances and influence, reshaping the geopolitical landscape.

Considering energy independence and alternative fuels, we explore how the shift away from oil payments in U.S. dollars could incentivize the U.S. to develop alternative energy sources and reduce its dependence on oil. This could have significant implications for the energy sector and investment patterns, potentially leading to a restructuring of the industry.

Investigating the impact on the U.S. trade balance and current account deficit, we find that the change in oil payment currencies could have a substantial effect. This shift may result in a trade imbalance and increase the current account deficit, creating economic challenges for the U.S. economy.

We also analyze the potential effects on inflation and consumer prices in the U.S. as a result of changing oil payment currencies. The findings suggest that the shift could lead to inflationary pressures and potentially impact consumer prices, posing challenges for policymakers.

Examining the potential consequences on U.S. stock markets and investment flows, we discover that the shift away from the U.S. dollar could introduce volatility and uncertainty. This may affect investment decisions and create new risks in the financial markets.

Furthermore, we explore the role of the Federal Reserve in managing the U.S. economy during the transition to alternative oil payment currencies. The findings highlight the importance of effective monetary policy and coordination to navigate potential disruptions.

Analyzing the impact on economic sanctions and global influence, we discover that the use of alternative oil payment currencies could impact the effectiveness of U.S. economic sanctions and potentially diminish its global influence.

Finally, we investigate the potential risks and challenges posed by a shift away from the U.S. dollar as the dominant currency for oil payments, including currency wars and financial instability. The findings emphasize the need for careful planning and coordination to mitigate these risks.

Overall, "The Dollar's Decline" provides a comprehensive analysis of the implications of shifting oil payments on the U.S. economy. It underscores the need for policymakers, economists, and politicians to closely monitor and prepare for potential disruptions and opportunities that may arise from this significant shift.

Implications for economists and politicians

As the world's oil payments shift away from the U.S. dollar and towards other currencies, economists and politicians must grapple with several significant implications. This subchapter explores the various consequences that this shift may have on the U.S. economy, global power dynamics, energy independence, trade balance, inflation, stock markets, monetary policy, energy sector restructuring, economic sanctions, and financial stability.

One of the key areas of concern is the impact on the U.S. dollar value and its position as the global reserve currency. Analyzing the effect of shifting oil payments on the value of the U.S. dollar is crucial for economists and politicians to understand the potential consequences for international trade, foreign exchange rates, and the U.S. economy's overall stability.

Furthermore, the geopolitical implications of this shift are significant. Examining the potential consequences on U.S. foreign relations and global power dynamics when oil is no longer paid in U.S. dollars is vital for policymakers to navigate potential changes in alliances, influence, and global economic order.

The shift in oil payments currencies could also incentivize the U.S. to develop alternative energy sources and reduce dependence on oil. Economists and politicians need to explore how this transition could impact the energy sector, investment patterns, and the pursuit of energy independence.

Additionally, investigating the impact on the U.S. trade balance and current account deficit when oil payments are no longer denominated in U.S. dollars is crucial for policymakers to understand potential effects on imports, exports, and overall economic stability.

Another crucial consideration is the potential effects on inflation and consumer prices in the U.S. as a result of changing oil payment currencies. Analyzing these effects will help economists and politicians understand how the shift may impact the cost of living and overall economic well-being.

Examining the potential consequences on U.S. stock markets and investment flows when the world's oil is no longer paid in U.S. dollars is also essential to understand potential risks and opportunities for investors and economic growth.

Moreover, analyzing the role of the Federal Reserve in managing the U.S. economy during the transition to alternative oil payment currencies is crucial for policymakers to develop effective monetary policies and ensure economic stability during this period of change.

Exploring potential changes in the U.S. energy sector and investment patterns resulting from shifting oil payment currencies is vital for economists and politicians to understand the long-term implications on employment, infrastructure, and energy security.

Furthermore, examining how the use of alternative oil payment currencies could impact the effectiveness of U.S. economic sanctions and its global influence is crucial for policymakers to assess potential vulnerabilities and adapt their strategies accordingly.

Lastly, investigating the potential risks and challenges posed by a shift away from the U.S. dollar as the dominant currency for oil payments, including currency wars and financial instability, is essential for economists and politicians to develop strategies to mitigate these risks and maintain global economic stability.

In conclusion, the implications for economists and politicians stemming from the shift in oil payments away from the U.S. dollar are vast and require careful analysis and consideration. Understanding the potential consequences on various aspects of the economy and global power dynamics is crucial for policymakers to navigate this transition effectively and ensure the continued stability and prosperity of the United States.

Recommendations for future research and policy-making

As the world shifts away from using U.S. dollars for oil payments and adopts alternative currencies, it is crucial for researchers and policymakers to delve into the various aspects and implications of this transition. By conducting further research and formulating effective policies, economists and politicians can better understand and navigate the potential impacts on the U.S. economy and global power dynamics. The following recommendations outline key areas that require further investigation:

1. What Happens to the U.S. Economy when the World's Oil is No Longer Paid with U.S. Dollars But With Other Currencies?

- Research should focus on analyzing the macroeconomic effects on the U.S. economy, including GDP growth, employment, and income distribution.

- Policymakers should consider the need for diversifying the economy and reducing dependence on oil revenues.

2. Impact on the U.S. dollar value: Analyzing the effect of shifting oil payments on the value of the U.S. dollar and its position as a global reserve currency.

- Researchers should study the potential consequences on exchange rates, monetary policy, and international trade.

- Policymakers need to assess strategies to maintain the stability and attractiveness of the U.S. dollar in a changing oil payment landscape.

3. Geopolitical implications: Examining the potential consequences on U.S. foreign relations and global power dynamics when oil is no longer paid in U.S. dollars.

- In-depth research should explore the geopolitical shifts that may arise from alternative currency arrangements and their impact on U.S. influence.

- Policymakers should consider adapting diplomatic and economic strategies to maintain U.S. global leadership.

4. Energy independence and alternative fuels: Exploring how the shift away from oil payments in U.S. dollars could incentivize the U.S. to develop alternative energy sources and reduce dependence on oil.

- Researchers should investigate the potential for increased investments in renewable energy, technological advancements, and energy diversification.

- Policymakers need to promote policies and incentives that support the transition to alternative fuels and reduce reliance on oil.

5. Trade balance and current account deficit: Investigating the impact on the U.S. trade balance and current account deficit when oil payments are no longer denominated in U.S. dollars.

- Research should examine the potential effects on exports, imports, and the overall balance of trade.

- Policymakers should consider policies to mitigate any negative impacts on trade imbalances.

6. Inflation and consumer prices: Analyzing the potential effects on inflation and consumer prices in the U.S. as a result of changing oil payment currencies.

- Researchers should assess the impact on domestic prices, inflation expectations, and overall economic stability.

- Policymakers need to monitor price dynamics and implement appropriate measures to mitigate inflationary pressures.

7. Stock market and investment implications: Examining the potential consequences on U.S. stock markets and investment flows when the world's oil is no longer paid in U.S. dollars.

- Research should investigate the potential effects on stock market performance, investor sentiment, and capital flows.

- Policymakers should consider measures to ensure the resilience and attractiveness of U.S. capital markets.

8. Federal Reserve and monetary policy: Analyzing the role of the Federal Reserve in managing the U.S. economy during the transition to alternative oil payment currencies.

- Researchers should assess the implications for monetary policy, including interest rates, money supply, and exchange rate management.

- Policymakers need to adapt the Federal Reserve's toolkit and communication strategies to navigate the changing landscape.

9. Energy sector restructuring: Exploring the potential changes in the U.S. energy sector and investment patterns resulting from shifting oil payment currencies.

- Research should focus on understanding the implications for energy companies, job creation, and infrastructure investments.

- Policymakers should promote policies that support a smooth transition and encourage sustainable energy practices.

10. Economic sanctions and global influence: Examining how the use of alternative oil payment currencies could impact the effectiveness of U.S. economic sanctions and its global influence.

- Research should assess the potential challenges and limitations of economic sanctions in a multi-currency oil payment system.

- Policymakers need to reassess the effectiveness of sanctions and explore alternative tools for exerting influence.

11. Currency wars and financial instability: Investigating the potential risks and challenges posed by a shift away from the U.S. dollar as the dominant currency for oil payments, including currency wars and financial instability.

- Research should analyze the potential for increased currency volatility, competitive devaluations, and financial contagion.

- Policymakers need to monitor and address emerging risks to financial stability through international cooperation and regulatory frameworks.

By addressing these research and policy gaps, economists and politicians can make informed decisions and develop strategies to navigate the changing landscape of oil payments and their implications for the U.S. economy and global power dynamics.